The King Is Here

Wyatt is my name, but you can call me Kickin' King,
My cuts are on time, and my rhymes will sting.
So please oh please, if you aren't my kind,
Don't take an amateur and blow his mind.
'Cause if you do, then he might think,
That you have the rhymes that are unique.
So don't try to dis me, try to be my friend,
'Cause if you do, you'll get yours in the end.
'Cause this is the business that I am in,
Kickin' King cuttin' rhymes again and again.
See I don't flip, and I don't flop,
'Cause I'm a mean go-getter, and I can't be dropped.
On *The Gong Show*, you won't be gonged,
'Cause it's Wyatt or Mr. King, not Cheech and Chong.
I'm not black; I'm white as milk,
My hair's not rough; it's smooth as silk.
I'm talkin' to parents, peers, and my friends,
I'm sorry, party people, but this is the end.
I'm tellin' you now that I'm for real,
'Cause I'm from Tennessee. What part? Nashville!

Only Halfway There

We were almost halfway there,
And then it finishes in thin air.
And when you go from the corner,
Your soul is seen by french horner.
That is deeper than the oceans,
And at the end of locomotions.
Tear your face from your skull,
And your mind has just been null.
Your stomach turns as if to hurl,
Your every toe about to curl.
It will unhinge your every nerve,
'Cause life is just one big curve.
I'll reach in and tear out your heart,
Because I'm just a stinking fart.
I take joy in others' pain,
It makes me dance in the rain.
Why the ache makes me smile,
I like the pain and for a while.
Am I weird? Well, that is true,
And I will laugh when I get blue.
I'd rip off my arm if I could feel,
All the pain of a dying seal.
Halfway there is where we started,
But I became really evilhearted!

Getting a Clear Conscious

For all the hurtful things that I said,
And all the tears I made you shed.
I take them back from your heart,
Just you read this is your part.
I don't expect you to forgive,
And I don't know how long we'll live.
But I must put my mind at ease,
It will help my heart if you please.
Just remember all the good,
And hope I did all I should.
If I don't get the chance to say,
Just know how sorry I am today.
I don't want to take a chance,
And end up without our last dance.
So if you could watch this step,
If I hadn't said it, I couldn't have slept.
My apologies to all I've hurt,
Just wait your turn and keep on your shirt.
I'll try to get to each and every one,
Before the day comes I meet the Father and Son.
First to Janice, I tell you, Mom,
I say forgive me and just stay calm.

Then to John, you're my brother,
And I do love you like I do my mother.
Then to Kaleigh, I cut you deep,
I hope this helps you fall asleep.
Now to Courtney, I know you're hurt,
And for that, I feel like dirt.
To my Uncle D., we've always been friends,
And all my love my heart sends.
Now, Alan, I know you have ill feelings toward me,
But I hope in the end, I had best intentions, you'll see.
Cheyenne, I know you say there's no more to do,
Even so, I know deep down, you still think I'll keep hurting you.
I guess if I missed someone else I've hurt,
Just know my mind and heart feel like a jerk.
Just always know—you don't know what day,
That this jerk will have to pay.
It could be today, or it could be tomorrow,
But everyone knows I'm leaving with lots of sorrow.
So this is farewell from Mr. King,
You will no longer hear me sing!

At the Brink of the End

Things in my life are turning upside down,
And I am starting to show it by my constant frown.
I know if I owned a gun, it would end today,
'Cause it feels like most don't care no matter what you say.
I say I go by proof 'cause that's how much you care,
I only have a handful of people who show love is in the air.
There are quite a few who like to beat me down,
Never tell me I do good things—just makes me feel like a clown.
If it wasn't for the few people who tell me the good I do,
My life would be over, and no one could walk in my shoes.
I got to do what they want me to, and they ain't gonna wait,
And I'm a jerk who doesn't do anything if I'm a second late.
I try my best to be a good person and always help others,
But my good they don't recognize, and the hatred toward me, it smothers.
No matter what I do, it gets thrown in my face and told it's wrong,
I try and try to do what's right, but told I can't, it's the same ole song.
So if one day I'm not around and you wonder what has happened,
I probably abandoned ship 'cause there's no ship that I'm the captain!

Listen

Why won't they listen when I say I'm hurting,
Why won't they listen when I say I'm in pain,
Why won't they listen when I say I can't take any more,
Why won't they listen when I say this ain't a game.
Why won't they listen when I say I need help,
Why won't they listen when I say I am broke,
Why won't they listen when I say don't leave me,
Why won't they listen when I say it ain't a joke.

What Am I?

I'm what they call a disabled vet,
If you live in America, there's plenty you've met.
And if you've ever wondered just what one really is,
I think all Americans should make it their biz.
So let's get started from one who knows firsthand,
'Cause I don't believe no one person should keep their head in the sand.
It's a person, whether female or male,
Who served their country, whether or not overseas, what the hell.
They volunteer their time away from family and friends,
And then they got the shaft in the very end.
They are injured for life—physical, mental, or both,
Yet they still love and honor their country so don't dis it this take note.
They can never work again, so they stay home and go mad,
And wait—I'm not finished if you think that isn't bad.
You do, however, get a small monthly check,
So most of you think it's okay—what the heck?
You'll all of a sudden think you have a lot of friends,
But every veteran finds that this one offends.
See, most believe that loyalty means true no matter what,
No arguments, decision made, case closed, no ifs, ands, or buts.
But every disabled veteran finds out really fast,
That people are only their friend when that monthly check is cashed.

But when they are in pain and distraught the rest of the month,
Everyone they ask for help from will act like a punk.
Then everyone wonders, "Why are they always crying?"
It's because people like you always say, "I don't have the time."

Assurance You're Still the Best

As everyone is waiting for holiday cheer,
You are concentrating on a more special day that's near.
Well, I am letting you know that I, too, think the same,
That today's very special to me 'cause it's the day I gave you your name.
Yes, your birthday is what I'm talkin' about—twenty-five years,
You are the first reason in my life for true joyful tears.
I dreamed and imagined what it would be like,
To have a little girl, and even at twelve, I knew I was right.
For nine years, I planned for your very special day,
And when it came, I adored my daddy's girl—you were the best in
    every single way.
You have always been the best to me,
Daddy's girl you've always been—it's plain to see.
So have a happy birthday and know this one fact,
You'll always be Daddy's girl to me in my heart, and that's that.
You're beautiful and smart and successful like I knew you would,
So please forgive me, Kaleigh Dawn King, for our last conversation
    because only you could!

A Reason to Feel Complete

I've said it twice before—first in '98 and again in '03,
But in case you don't remember, you deserve to hear it again from me.
You were the third child of mine, and that made my life complete,
'Cause even though I was already blessed with two little girls, having
    my own Harley, I knew would be neat.
Yeah, at first, we were not exactly sure whether girl or boy,
With a name like Harley, the only problem I thought would be when
    I'd buy you a toy.
But let me inform you now and straight from my heart,
You turned out great and exactly who was meant to be from the start.
So don't ever think I wanted you to be anyone or anything different
    than who you are.
'Cause God created you perfect, and to prove it, I'm paying to name
    you a star.
Yes, you heard me right, I meant like in the sky,
And I will try to explain it to you exactly why.
Well, remember the day we looked and were amazed
At the solar eclipse as we shared together and gazed.
Well, you remember how remarkable we thought it was,
Well, when I think about the peace you bring me, that's what my
    heart does.
I hope you now know how important this day is to me,
And I hope you have the best birthday ever, my Harley!

My Goddess Daya

So, my goddess, you are forty-seven,
And you have put me in heaven.
To me, your body is like thirty-four,
It keeps me always asking for more.
And your soul is like twenty-three,
And was fashioned just for me.
But our bond is so very strong,
That we'll be together for a hundred years long.
No one will ever tear us apart,
'Cause our love for each other is straight from the heart.
If someone tries to extinguish our light,
That's when they will have a really huge fight.
'Cause we are already one—that's all I need to say,
Except I love you and happy birthday!

My Heart for Daddy's Girl

Today my daddy's girl is twenty-six,
And this is for your birthday fix.
I hope your day is going well,
'Cause you're the best—isn't that swell?
I love you to the moon
And hope to see you very soon.
You should know that you are great.
So happy birthday—and I'm not late.
Kaleigh Dawn, your dad sends wishes,
To let you know that it's you he misses.

Try to Stop True Love

So I know it's been hard this year with me,
The ups and the downs—but I hope you're happy.
I won't share your age for the world to know,
But I will share that you have helped me to grow.
I will try to help the next be better than the last,
And if no one likes that, they can eat trash.
You are my goddess, even my priestess,
And I will always think that you are the neatest.
So have a happy birthday from your priest,
'Cause you are the most awesome, to say the least.
This may be corny, but it's the best I can do,
And no one in this world is as talented as you.
Now happy birthday, Shirley Wiser, I hope it is clear,
That you're the only one that I want near!

A New Start from the Heart

I no longer refer to you as my little poppins 'cause you're an adult,
But I'm not sure what to call you now, and many reasons are the result.
One, because you're married, but he seems to be a good man,
Another is now you're a mother, but you seem to have a good plan.
But the most important reason is because I don't know who you are now,
Which really breaks my heart, and I'd change this if you told me how.
'Cause to me, you are still Daddy's little poppin,
Even though you're twenty, married, a mother—that's never stoppin'.
You're wonderful and smart and deserve everything,
And no matter what, forever your praises will I sing.
So whatever you want or need from your dad, just ask,
And I will do my best to make it happen, no matter how hard the task.
But I hope your birthday today is well,
Because I love you, and you deserve it more than words can tell!

The Way I Am

My heart lights up when love is around,
And my goddess has it, and it abounds.
This world mostly has a heart that is cold,
And my honesty is nothing but bold.
Most can't take me because of this fact,
What I say is always nothing but exact.
I don't hold back about how I feel,
But you can guarantee I'm the one who is real.
Loyalty is something I hold as dear,
There is nothing or no one that I fear.
I will never ever turn on a friend,
I will have their back till the end.
Toe-to-toe, face-to-face, we will face it all,
Even if I have to get there at a crawl.
Don't ever cross me, or you will know,
Just what I'm made of when I decide to go.
And if you hurt a friend of mine,
I will no longer insist on being kind.
I flip a switch for those I choose to care about,
My love and honor is always truly devout.
Don't ever get confused about my age and size,
If you cross the line, I will still cross your tees and dot your eyes.

Death Has Knocked at My Door

Death is at the door, and I don't really care,
'Cause I'm stuck in jail, and it really ain't fair.
And I am actually innocent even though that is rare,
And I don't have much more that I am willing to share.
To get out of here, I'd agree to go anywhere,
I need to go to the VA 'cause I am really scared.
Stuck here forever with no hope of getting out,
I asked for a bond, but there is still no amount.
This is all so messed up, and I don't know what to do,
I really can't do nothing; I don't know about you.
Can anyone hear my plea? Can anyone hear me scream?
I just want to wake up from this god-awful dream.
My life has turned to darkness—they've taken away my world,
My brain and heart have stopped, and my body has finally curled!

handwritten: obit Known as "Wolf"

handwritten: LA Vergne TN Dade Wayne Burton Sr died 2022 51 yrs old wife Tina + 7 sons + 2 girls

My Hero

You walked with me from the time I was a child,
Some said we were evil; some said we were wild.
You always had my back everywhere we would go,
What comes next, I just wanna know.
They call you Wolf, and you called me Hawk—how cool,
And the one thing you liked was the golden rule.
Always be REAL—don't act like a zero,
That's why you were always my hero.
We've never failed to remain friends throughout time,
Now let me tell you 'cause it's been one heck of a climb.
We've had more ups than we've had downs,
Boy, how they've all tried to make us look like clowns.
Then God stepped in and brought you a woman straight from above,
So you decided to show only one your undying love.
So I said, "God, if my hero can have this, would you give it to me?"
Then I met a woman, and God said, "Here's your Shirley."
And at least before God took you, you got to know,
That I get to be happy before I die just like my hero!
RIP Dade Wayne "Wolf" Burton

handwritten: Not sure if friend or his dad.

Why Be Crooked

You don't have to be like that, especially with me,
'Cause I am the most generous you can easily see.
I give until my money is gone, and that's true,
What more do you expect me to do?
I only ask for loyalty and respect—that is all,
But instead, everyone around here sets me up for a fall.
Y'all are out for yourselves no matter who goes down,
You always try to make the innocent look like a clown.
Go to any lengths even if against the law,
Acting how you want as if no one ever saw.
It starts from the top and goes all through the legal teams,
It's got me to the point where everyone can hear my screams.
I now hate this county, and I can't wait to get out,
But I keep it all inside 'cause it does no good to sit and pout.
So I'm letting everyone know if you come here just beware,
Coffee County is so crooked, and you can smell it in the air.
So brace yourself if you decide to come here,
The whole legal system is crooked, and so are the others, and it's perfectly clear.

Beaten by a Burton

You may not know this, but I'm a Burton by blood,
But I guarantee you know all the Burtons are tough.
My great-grandfather was Cherokee and had only one arm.
The fact he could knock out a mule with one punch sends alarm.
My grandfather Bob Burton was a navy boxer,
And besides being mean, he was a ship sleepwalker.
So when he got out, he tried to be a cop.
They said you can't knock them out, but he wouldn't stop.
His boss said, "Try, arrest them, be reasonable."
But of course, he's a Burton, so he said, "That's not feasible."
Then he decided to be a pastor, so he and his brothers built a church,
With all the things he could do, that's where he stopped his search.
Now because he was a Burton, he demanded the whole family to go,
And this was not the time to let the Burton's stubbornness to show.
But he had the best of intentions; he just wanted us all to live right,
And he was gonna do what God asked even if it meant a fight.
Now he stands behind those gates and welcomes us one by one,
And we are all glad; he was a Burton, son of a gun.
Then there was my uncle Steve, a Burton through and through,
Another one that when he barked, you did what he said to do.
But like the rest of us in the end, he kneeled to God,
And with his dying breath, he took God's hand with a smile and a nod!

The Letdown Is My Life

I'm always helping others all across the land,
But nowhere can I find a real friend.
You hate me or love me; there's no doubt.
Most don't know what I'm talkin' about.
Each day that goes by, I get the letdown of my life.
Even though I don't want it, I have to deal with a lot of strife.
I'm always looking for my golden buzzer,
But I want the world to love each other.
If you plan to let me down or even hold me back,
Your card will end up at the bottom of the stack.
I look to the clouds for my silver lining,
'Cause I have a place that inside I'm designing.
There's peace love and freedom alike,
But so far all, I get is a letdown that is my life!

You're Easy to Love

So, sweetheart, I hear that you're twenty-eight,
And facts are facts so that you can't debate.
But your heart and spirit put you at forty,
And because of that, I know you won't get this distorted.
You have a heart of gold and have become family,
Not by blood or by marriage but by who you be.
Most don't realize or recognize all you do,
But the ones in this family know it's true.
You get knocked around a lot and usually turn your head,
But I think you know if you asked us we'd take them to the shed.
We got your back, Andrea, and you know this,
'Cause you are real and such a sweet miss.
Ever since I've met you, I liked you a lot,
And you don't get shown enough that you are quite hot.
So hold your head up, and you'll get your day,
And those who hurt you—they will pay.
I can't tell you enough; you're easy to love,
And you back those you care about when push comes to shove.
And that's what makes you a beautiful woman
And as long as I'm alive, you'll have a happy birthday from now on!

You're the Light in My Tunnel

Well, bro, guess what? You're now forty-five,
And because of family and God, you're still alive.
And I'm glad you are, and this is why,
Because now you're a role model, and that's no lie.
Little ET looks up to you,
And Jeannie loves being the miss of your crew.
I'm so glad you've become so strong,
You've turned around your whole life, and it didn't take long.
Soon for your family, you'll buy a home,
So y'all don't have to live like me and, from place to place, roam.
I'm so proud of how well you have done,
And to me, little bro, you're the wiser one.
I know you'll continue to lead the way,
So be with God and bless you and happy birthday.

My Complete Turnaround

Today I'm starting a fresh life,
Hopefully soon, I'll have a new wife.
And I will finally end all my strife,
Because disloyalty and, dishonor cut like a knife.
All of my pain and sorrow will go away,
While peace and harmony are here to stay.
And I will serve God—come what may,
And from now on, it will be a brighter day.
The path I'll be walking will be brand-new,
And I'll be walking with God here in a few.
And He will tell me just what to do,
I just have to follow His cue.
I only have to trust in the Lord
And live my life in one accord.
Straying to the left or right, I can't afford,
He will lead me through the right door.
Because I will put all my trust in Him,
And my life will have me out on a limb.
This all seems so very slim,
Like a tire on a car without a rim.
But don't get me wrong, I know what I owe,
And keeping my word, I always show.
And I'll stand face-to-face and toe-to-toe,
And my answer to evil will always be no!

Go the Right Direction

Where do we go now in our life?
I'll be your husband, and you'll be my wife.
Together we'll get rid of all strife,
Use our hearts and put away the knife,
As long as we stay true to ourselves
And put the past up on the shelf.
We can still turn our life to God,
So that in the end, we can be where angels trod.
First, we need to find our own home
So that we no longer have to roam.
Living with others is really a drag
Or having to live out of a bag.
We'll find a church that we can attend
So that our hearts we can mend.
We should try to get closer to each other,
Especially since you might be a new mother.
I can't wait to help you raise a child
And lessen my temper to only mild.
But we must stay true to ourselves for real,
And there must be nothing that we try to conceal.
Honesty is as important as love,

Working together on all important stuff.
Making a home as a family as well,
If we have a problem we need to tell.
So where we go from here is up to us,
As long as we do it tougher with no fuss.

Take a Leap of Faith

After you know a person, you can love a person,
'Cause when you actually know a person, then you can show a person.
You can show love, joy, and peace,
Understanding long-suffering and true release.
All the fruits of the Spirit, if you please,
Kind, good, faithful, and gentle on your knees.
The Holy Spirit has what's good for you,
Removing sinful nature is what He will do.
And I promise in the end, it's what you will love too,
Then your whole life will be renewed.
You will see things start to get better,
And soon you will show others to the letter.
And maybe for others to be a trendsetter,
And God will take notice that you're a go-getter.

The Heartbeat of My Life

When I'm with you, there's no pain, and I'm never sick,
And you are the one who makes my heart tick.
You are the reason I want to be me,
'Cause you see all the good that no one can see.
You make everything in life like the sun so bright,
When my life was at its darkest, you showed me the light.
With you, I'm guaranteed to have a beautiful world.
Your heart makes me smile, and your love makes my toes curl.
Yes, it's true that one day soon, you will be my wife,
But you always have and always will be the heartbeat of my life!

You Are My True Heart

You know we first met on Valentine's 2021,
We've always found a way, no matter what, to have fun.
I've seen you at a friend's house while I was playing pool,
I knew right away that being with you would be cool.
We like to have fun, fishing and cooking,
Crystal, you are to me the girl who's the best looking.
Our nine-year-old Laila helps keep us bonded together.
JR will be your man, sweetheart, no matter what the weather.
I plan to take you to Ireland and fulfill your every need,
'Cause I know that's your dream and winning your love is just my speed.
So I hope to marry you one day, my sweet girl,
And I'm hoping you'll say yes and give us a whirl.
So I hope you see now that my heart for you is true,
Just remember, come what may that I always will love you.
From Wallace Potter (JR)
To Crystal Shilling

Corruption Hell

Here I am again in Coffee County jail,
And I am starting to feel I'm being put through hell.
I don't understand why an easy case takes so long,
My lawyer never visits, but I try to stay strong.
The legal system here is corrupt to make a long story short,
And there seems to be no justice in this Mickey Mouse court.
I'll get out one day—that is a fact,
And I'm leaving this county, but where? I don't know exactly.
Any place else is better than here,
Coffee County is hell, and that much is clear!

To Infinity and Beyond

I have a best friend; her name is Shirley Wiser,
And I hope we're tougher until I'm an old miser.
She's there for me in the good times and the bad,
She makes me smile and hardly ever gets mad.
She knows how to love even when I don't deserve it,
She holds my heart and knows how to preserve it.
I can't wait to see where our future will go,
'Cause I know for a fact that I love her so.
I found my diamond in the rough, and I know I'm not wrong,
'Cause we love each other to infinity and beyond!

So Shall It Be

When I was forty, I got a wife.
Then I got locked up, and they gave me life.
Then soon after I went to jail,
She started sleeping with my best friend, Mel.
Here I thought I'd be married long,
But I married a whore, so I was wrong.
I know if I get out that I'll be back,
'Cause I'll kill them both, and that's a fact.
Maybe if I do my time, all will be well,
They'll die of old age, and karma will prevail.

Deep Consideration

Look up to our Lord who rules the earth and sky,
'Cause He is the One who will get us by.
Even though we continue to daily ask why,
All of our excuses for our actions don't fly.
Think before you act, and you will see,
What kind of person you should be.
Search your soul and test your heart,
And you will find our Lord will not part.
No matter how it feels, He did not hide,
In that dark desert, He was by your side.
Open your ears and open your eyes,
'Cause it's the devil that is the father of lies!

The Insanity of It All

Life is leaving this immortal soul,
My surroundings are taking its toll.
People's thoughts are impeding my mind,
My heart is feeling like it's no longer kind.
I don't seem like the same person no more,
I'm not really sure what I'm fighting for.
There seems like no hope of leaving this place,
It's like I'm coming in last in this cat-and-mouse race.
I keep wishing for this torture of my heart and mind to end,
Yet it feels like death is coming closer to being my friend.
I keep looking for the light at the end of the road,
But I don't think any longer I can carry this load!

A True Look at Reason

What part of no do we not understand?
What part of yes will guide our hand?
What part of up will keep your mind sound?
What part of down plants your feet on the ground?
Do we know the real reason for all of our strife?
Discover your soul and discover the meaning of your life.
Once you do that, what's in your heart will appear,
And the true look at reason will finally be clear!

My Vow to Shirley

So you are the light that I'm looking for,
That's what gives me hope I'll go out the door.
So every day that goes by, I wait for them to say,
King, pack your stuff and be on your way.
Down the stairs, up front, and then out the gate,
I've already called you, so on you, I now wait.
We'll start a fresh life far away from here,
'Cause this county is our problem; this has been made clear.
You're my diamond eyes, and I'm your papa bear,
You are all I think of, and for you, I truly care.
Don't think for a moment I care about anything else,
Not drugs, not women—I love you more than myself,
I will always love you to infinity and beyond,
I give you my word, and this is my bond.
I know for a fact that we are meant to be,
So no more talking, instead I'll let you see!

A True Blessing to Me

It's now been three years since you warmed my heart,
I asked for your hand so we'd never part.
And much to my surprise, you told me yes,
Although the past decade of my life was a mess.
Ever since that day, my life's turned around,
And I know for sure my soulmate I've found.
I look forward to the day when we're hand in hand,
When you are my lady, and I am your man.
We'll grow old together to the end of our days,
And never have to worry about ever parting ways.
You are my lover, and with you, I'm never sad,
And the most awesome woman I've ever had.
I can't thank God enough for the blessing He's given,
'Cause you have truly made my life finally worth livin'.
Our love will fly high where the eagles soar,
Happy anniversary, I will always be yours!

What's Inside

The pain and darkness within my heart,
In this state of depression is where it did start.
I can't let none of it ever be seen,
None would ever know what I mean.
I couldn't ever make my true feelings clear,
Nor would anyone try to really hear.
Plus, I can never really shed a tear,
So I try not to let anyone near
I keep all at a distance far away,
Never say anything with all that I say.
It's all a big secret that no one will know,
They can't see inside me no matter what I show!

Orange Slide Beasts

We got these things on our feet they call slides,
But they are not very comfortable rides.
Plus, they are orange and ugly as can be,
And cheap as well—it's plain to see.
You take a few laps and have holes in the sole,
And your feet for sure have taken a toll.
They tend to slide off when you're walking upstairs,
Hence the word *slides*, but no one really cares.
In the shower, they protect you from all sorts of things,
'Cause athlete's foot, I tell you it really stings.
I guess it's better than nothing at all,
Coffee County orange slides, I hope you don't fall!

He's Going to the Feds

Our boy here is going to the federal pen,
We know because he tells us every now and then.
He doesn't really want to go to this place,
You can hear it in his voice and see it on his face.
When they decide to take him, he doesn't really care.
To get out of Coffee County, he'd rather be there.
Get to the pen and finish paying for his crime,
It's up in the air if he learns his lesson this time.
Once you're going feds, you surely will pay.
And usually to the courts, it doesn't matter what you say.
Will he change his ways to be determined when he gets out,
Return to a life of crime or go a different route!

That's of Today

She's an unsavory girl known as a that,
And being a virgin is something she is not.
Now I am not saying that she is not hot,
But her vagina probably has jungle rot.
You can't depend on her to be faithful at all,
But if you just want sex, she's the one to call.
Remember she will definitely sleep with your friend,
And most likely be a headache in the end.
Her personality sucks this is most likely true,
But you will never have to tell her the words *I love you*.
Be careful sleeping with her; you don't know what you'll catch,
'Cause I bet there's something lethal living in that snatch.
You better wear a raincoat—I tell ya this much, bro,
She gives a whole new meaning to the title hoe!

Rainbows Mean a Lot

Blue says that you are easily befriended.
Yellow says that you have peace that's never ended.
Green says that you are envied by everyone around.
Red says you give love by leaps and by bounds.
Brown says your mind is confused or torn.
Black says your soul is evil to the core.
Orange says you're lost and don't know where to go.
White says your heart is as pure as the snow.
Pink says everyone you meet is just so very cute.
Purple says you're musical, and your life is like a flute.
When you see a rainbow, it really means a lot.
Each and every color means more than you thought.
So next time you see someone, look really deep
And see if you can tell the color that they keep.
Also, this was God's way of saying this is through.
Never again will I ever do this to you!

Heart-to-Heart

Granny, I appreciate all the love that you show.
It means more to me than you will ever know.
I'm sorry it'll be a minute till we see each other again,
But I know our hearts will touch every now and then.
Because you have taught me about the Lord, and that is why I say,
That you are the reason that every day I pray.
I thank you for instilling the goodness in my heart,
Every morning I wake up, I think of you to start.
Every time I wonder how I will deal with all my strife,
That's when God reminds me it's because Granny is in your life!

From Justin Burnette
To Cordelia Burnette (Granny)

Purple Dinosaurs

Purple dinosaurs they say is a happy family,
This is just as silly as it can really be.
Think about the one that they call Barney,
They are up to something; this is plain to see.
I believe they are out to get our kid,
Throw them in a hole, and tightly seal the lid.
I mean whoever heard of a purple dinosaur,
That's like saying there is something as a decent faithful whore.
When I was asked my thoughts on them, this is what I said,
"Take all the purple dinosaurs and shoot them in the head!"

A Plea from My Heart

My mind is going blank, and I'm forgetting who I am.
My heart is losing hope because my life is in a jam.
I'm running from the darkness with all of my might,
Trying to find the true guiding light.
I'm afraid that if soon I don't get out of this place,
I'll be forever lost without even a trace.
Will anyone not help can anyone not see,
Exactly what this place is really doing to me?
Can anyone not see the void in my soul,
Or how my very spirit is no longer whole?
God, I now beg You if You truly do exist,
I might need something, but I do not need this.
I'll do what You ask if You'll just get me out.
I'll change all my ways; I'll go a different route.
I'll go to church every Sunday, and You know my word is my bond.
Just get me out of here, and my life is Yours, dear God!

Knowing My Path

I don't know what to do wandering around in my head,
Pondering where I've been recalling what I've said.
Figuring out the ones I followed and seeing where it's led,
Remembering all the joy and all the tears that have been shed.
Which direction is my life going from here,
I believe it is all beginning to come clear.
Will each day bring another reason to cheer?
Will I finally have peace with the one who is dear?
All that I know is that it's under control,
Because the One up above is running the show.
So all I have to do is go with the flow,
And in the end, God will keep all my ducks in a row!

I Love My Country

There are lots of beautiful places in this country to see,
With months of excitement, this I guarantee.
You can see them all at your own speed,
And return back home whenever you need.
Because as long as we don't destroy this great land,
These wonderful sites will always be at hand.
There's the Space Needle on Washington's Coast,
And in New York, Niagara Falls is the most.
Mount Rushmore in South Dakota is really cool,
And the Grand Canyon in Arizona is like a big empty pool.
The Statue of Liberty stands tall and proud,
And Mardi Gras is always really loud.
The Alamo in Texas is really swell,
Visit Universal Studios, and you'll have a story to tell.
Go all the way West, and you'll see the Pacific,
And all the way East, the Atlantic is just as terrific.
Disneyland is in California, which you'll like without a doubt,
And Disney World in Florida will give you something to smile about.
As you can see, this country is awesome—that's clear.
So go visit it all, and you'll have plenty to cheer!

My Love Is Deeper Than Words Can Say

You are the sunlight that outshines the rain.
You are the cure that removes all my pain.
You are the reason my mind stays sane.
You are the joy that helped me live again.
You are the peace that runs through my brain.
You are the pace car that keeps me in my lane.
You are the achievement that I want to attain.
You wash all my problems straight down the drain.
No one compares to the love you have shown.
When I look back at our life, my, how we have grown.
As long as we're together, we'll never be alone.
My love for you is always written in stone.
Our devotion to each other is a one-way zone.
Our loyalty to each other has been proven to the bone.
Don't ever forget how I feel about you.
I mean I walked sixty miles just to meet you—it's true.
Now my life's been made whole all the way through,
And the happiness we have every day is made new.
So the skies of our future are a brighter blue,
All those around us need to get a clue.

Because it's obvious by now we will never part.
We've been meant for each other from the very start.
And our love grows deeper, heart to heart.
You can see that our passion is off the chart.
For you and you only, I am fond,
To only your heartbeat do I respond.
You're the only swan in this great big pond,
And I love you to infinity and beyond!

The Prayer of a Contrite Spirit

Everything this county has done is not right,
And it seems like there is no end in sight.
Every day I pray the truth will come to light
Because more and more I am determined to win this fight.
All the facts are already written in black-and-white,
So as a soldier, I will continue to battle with all my might.
A guilty plea is something I simply refuse
Because with God on my side, how can I lose?
So it does not matter what they accuse,
The straight and narrow path is what I will choose.
With the Lord's help, I will show I have paid my dues,
And I have faith that soon they will come with good news.
"King, pack your stuff," is what they will say,
Walk me out the door and say have a nice day.
I will continue to serve God and not go astray,
With my nose in the Word, I will continue to pray.
This is my solemn vow I now give,
The Christian life is what I will live.
So I know that my life will be filled with joy and peace
Because I confess my sins to the Lord, and I feel the release.
I thank You, God, for Your love and Your grace,
And I thank You in advance that You got me out of this place.
And my entire past You chose to erase,
And that old man has left without a trace!

What's in Store in the End

It's true that you get exactly what you say,
Then tomorrow will be a brighter, sunnier day.
You should always search in life for a better way
Because whatever wrong you do, the piper you will pay.
If you look to the heavens for the Lord above,
He will share His grace and show you His love.
He will descend His spirit like a dove,
And I promise He'll fit your life like a glove.
The more you read His Word and pray without ceasing
And confess all your sins, then the more He'll release.
So you can start to feel more joy and more peace
Because our Lord is the One who will never tease.
Exactly what He says is exactly what He'll do,
And you can guarantee He is just and true.
What He does for one, He will also do for you,
And He will stand by your side until He sees you through.
You never have to doubt or worry if He's there,
Whenever you need Him, just say a simple prayer.
And on the Day of Judgment, you will meet Him in the air,
Then all of His blessings you will get to share!

This Is My True Birthday Wish for You

I know my baby is fifty years old,
"But you don't look your age" is what you've been told.
You know that you'll always be beautiful to me,
And soon you'll be my wife, and then you will see
Because you'll have my last name—this much is true,
You'll have my whole heart and benefits too.
Medical dental optical and scripts,
Military ID for all your post-trips.
Not only that, but you can also say you're my wife
And never be separated for life.
I could never ask for a better woman I say,
Because my life only gets better each and every day.
I'm so glad I found a person this great,
That I loved so dear from our very first date.
I hope you feel younger every year that goes by,
If I fail to make you feel that way just know that I try.
I'll never leave your side; my word is my bond.
So happy birthday, and I love you to infinity and beyond!

Keep Me Out of Your Mind

Walking the rock and biding my time,
Thinking about how to bust a new rhyme,
Digging holes deep but trying to climb,
If you want to pay me, put it on chime.
I'm not really worried what you have to say,
I'm living my life from day to day.
Just around the corner, I'll be on my way,
Coffee County ain't the place that I want to stay.
Be careful what you do to me,
My bad side ain't where you want to be.
Try it out, and you will see,
In the end, I will be free.
Murfreesboro is where I'm going to call home,
Roll a blunt and smoke it to the dome.
Rutherford County is where I will roam.
All you, fake people, can leave me alone
Because I am Wyatt, and there is no clone.
If I don't like you, then you're off my phone.
I got four daughters who are bad as hell.
You say that you want them, but I say, "Oh well."
They're off limits because from heaven, they fell.
Into the sunset, my ship will now sail!

That's Facts

See, I don't agree with all of these snitches.
If you do it to me, then I'll put you in ditches.
Because I've been taught that you should get stitches,
And me and Shirley remember we are witches.
If there is a battle, you'll find me in the trenches.
In the end, I'll get your attention.
So if you want to fight, I'm not the one,
I can guarantee it will be no fun.
I don't fight fair, and I'm good with a gun.
Plus, I will use anything under the sun.
And until you stop moving, I'm never done,
So your best bet is just to move on.
The reality is that I make a better friend,
And that will be the best benefit in the end.
All your hurts and troubles, I can help you mend,
Let's work together and start a new trend.
Peace and harmony is what I'd rather send,
A helping hand is what I like to lend.
But if you turn on me, then you will offend,
And into the heavens, I will make your soul ascend.
So let's all try to just get along,
Let's change all the rules and create a new song.

Roll a blunt and act like Cheech and Chong,
I have all the money, so I can't be wrong.
You should listen to me because I always keep it real,
I was raised in the projects of East Nashville.
When you get to know me, it seems so surreal.
I'll always back you up because loyal I am still.
The longer I am here, the more I want to leave,
How have I come to be so naive?
Not to know there's no honor amongst thieves,
All of my stress I need to relieve.
Getting to a higher plane is what I'm trying to achieve!

It's in My Head

I'm sitting in jail, and I'm known to have bars,
And most of the time, my head is in the stars.
When I'm on the street, I can buy all the cars,
All the time I did; I was never in wars.
Now every month, I get the biggest checks.
When my girl walks the streets, she's causing wrecks.
Because she and her daughter—they got back,
And I am the one who has the big stack.
If you hang with me, you'll have no lack,
And I buy those guns that go *clack, clack*.
My loyalty is guaranteed to be the best,
And my honesty, of course, is better than the rest.
My honor and my pride are something you can't test,
How I please women is like a cardiac arrest.
Going down the road with my girl in my hand,
Sitting on the beach with my feet in the sand.
Sipping lemonade and playing in the band,
I love my country on the Constitution I stand.
Just to break it down, let me make it clear,
I only tell the truth and put a bug in your ear.
If you mess with my people, I will give you a tear.
Bring something to the table or don't come near.

Don't make us put you down like a rifle to a deer.
Like my army unit, we have no fear.
Why can't everyone keep it all real?
When it comes to me, you will know how I feel.
I don't lie, I don't cheat, and I don't steal.
If you think that I won't, then I tell you I will.
Don't mess with me because I'm from East Nashville!

Mine Eyes Have Seen the Glory

O Lord of lords and King of kings,
Won't You show me what this next year brings?
I worship You and You alone,
And I know one day, You'll get me home.
I may not know the time or day,
But I trust Your word anyway.
Show me mercy and give me hope,
I know You'll give me strength so I can cope.
My whole household will serve You for the rest of my life,
My mother, my grandmother, and my new wife.
I've seen the error of my ways; this is true,
And I will obey what You ask me to do.
I'll go to Bible college and live a life that's pure,
And get my minister's license this is for sure.
I'll lead souls to You; there is no doubt,
Because now the steps of my path are on a new route.
I've finally woken up, and my mind is clear,
Your voice Lord is the one I hear.
All I have to do is put my faith in You.
Everything will be fine because I finally have a clue.
So if you really want your whole life to go right,
Just believe the love of God is dynamite.

He'll walk you through hard times and never steer you wrong,
If you put your faith and trust in Him your whole life long.
But you must remember faith without works is dead,
So you must always continue to do what you said.
I will live a righteous life and follow God's call,
And only through repentance will I continue not to fall.
Open my eyes and ears so I can see and hear what You say.
God, I ask for Your help in Jesus's name, I pray!

AMEN!

The Truth Is Good News

For peace and understanding are what I do ask,
But to accept those things is no easy task.
Joy is something I look for each day.
Take my heart, dear Lord, and show me the way.
If you follow Him, He'll show you the right path.
But if you blaspheme Him, He'll show you His wrath.
Choose to serve Him, and He never will leave.
There's a time to rejoice and a time to grieve.
Yes, it's true. We are all born sinners,
We repent and walk true, so we end as winners.
Faith and hope are what God likes to see,
But the greatest is love for you and for me.
The Scriptures say, "Be patient and endure to the end,"
And to help with this, His Holy Spirit he will send.
Having a partner will help you serve the Lord,
But three who stick together are as strong as a triple-braided cord.
When two or more agree, the Lord is in the midst,
And even the devil has to flee when you resist.
With faith as small as a mustard seed, the mountain must obey,
So you really must listen to what God has to say.
Preach God to all the earth so that all will change their tune,
So the Scriptures are fulfilled, and He comes for us soon!

Oh, What a Feeling

Can you feel the presence of the Lord?
You can ask Him in your heart—Will you open up the door?
All you have to do is ask Him to come in.
You may have done it once, but you can always do it again.
Just tell Him you repent and then change your ways.
Invite the Holy Spirit like in Pentecostal days.
You will never be sorry; this I guarantee,
Because your life will be the greatest it could ever be.
Put your faith and trust in God from the heavens above.
He will show you all His mercy, and you will feel all His love.
Everything will get better; you will never be the same.
You will see if you're blind, and you will walk if you're lame.
He heals the brokenhearted and makes the deaf hear.
He will always have your back so you never have to fear.
He's better than prudential—on the solid rock, you'll stand.
When you're walking through the valley, He lends a helping hand.
You never have to worry if you'll make it through,
Because in the name of Jesus, what He says is what He'll do!

Peace in My Heart

Hauling a load down the road of redemption,
Praying to the Lord, and giving up superstition.
I already know where this road will lead to,
Heaven above, Lord, I'm coming to be with You.
I throw up my hands and pray in the Spirit.
A clean white robe is now that all will fit.
No temptation Satan get behind me,
I love Jesus, and His ways are all I see.
On my way to that pearly white gate,
This world of sin is all that I hate.
Then one day, I'll walk those streets of gold,
Because the Lord's nail-scarred hands are now what I hold.
Lead me, Lord, walk with me today.
Walk me down that path away from all dismay.
I will honor Your Word and obey all Your commands.
I pray for Your blessings, and on the solid rock, I stand.
Lord, show me Your power and show me Your grace.
Open up these doors and get me out of this place.
I will be Yours for the rest of my life.
You've taken all my sins and removed all my strife.
I give You all the glory the honor and the praise.
I dance before You, Lord, and holy hands I raise.
I've turned from my wicked ways, and my heart is Yours today.
My whole house will serve the Lord, and on the righteous path, I'll stay!

Faith-Filled Praise for Thankful Days

Now I lay me down to sleep,
I thank You, Lord. I'm Yours to keep.
I thank You for another day,
That's closer to me being on my way.
Your promises are true, and this I know,
And to Your people, You always show.
If we are faithful, You are true,
To bring us peace and bring us through.
So I thank You, Lord, for bringing peace,
And I thank You, Lord, for my release.
March 13 will soon be here,
Then my freedom will be clear.
That will be a glorious day,
In Jesus's name, this I pray!

AMEN!

I've Been Delivered, I've Been Set Free

I was headed for hell because of all my sins,
And one day, I felt conviction tug at my heart and then.
I prayed to God for repentance and for Jesus to save my soul,
And in His great mercy, He cleansed me and made me whole.
I felt His love fill me and start changing my evil ways,
Because right then, I decided to serve Him for the rest of my days.
The blood of Jesus saved me from all my iniquity,
And I felt His awesome power and knew I had been set free.
He started healing my body, my heart, my soul, and my mind,
And then He filled me with His spirit like one of a kind.
Now I plan to serve Hirn with all of my heart,
Because He chose to love me from the very start.
I would have done this years ago, but I didn't have a clue,
But now I've been delivered and know exactly what to do!

Psalms 34

A Wish from My Heart to Yours

Valentine's Day is the reason for everyone to be sweet,
To give a piece of your heart to everyone that you meet.
But there's always that special someone who everyone holds so dear,
That's the one you give your whole heart to just to make that clear.
Shirley, you are my treasure to which I give the rest of my life,
And I hope and pray real soon I get to make you my wife.
If I ever get out of here, our life will be complete,
We can finally have a baby, Lord, won't that be neat?
We'll have a little us running around our home.
We can buy us an RV, so around this country, we can roam.
I wouldn't change a thing of our life together in any kind of way,
Except to have spent more time together so happy Valentine's Day.
I also want to say I'm sorry for anything I've done wrong.
Just know that I always have and always will love you to infinity and
    beyond!

More Than Enough

When I'm asked what's important, I say it's the cross.
It's where you need to go if you're broken or you're lost.
It will help heal your body; it will help heal your soul.
If you need to fix your finances, He will help meet your goal.
Read the Word of God and pray every day.
If you want to get to heaven, Jesus is the way.
When I think of love, I see His nail-scarred hands.
That's when I'm determined—on the solid rock, I stand.
So if you have a problem and you need to make it through,
Open up your heart and try to get a clue.
He said, "I love you all," with His arms open wide,
"And all you have to do is invite Me inside.
I want to be a friend to each and every one.
I don't discriminate; it doesn't matter what you've done.
Believe that you receive, and you'll get what you ask."
No matter what the problem, He's up to the task.
So when you come to Jesus for a healing touch,
Just look at the cross because He loved you this much!

The BIBLE

Yes, That's the Book for Me

The Word of God is truth from beginning to end.
It tells of our Redeemer who is also our Best Friend.
There is no one else in history who has shown so much love.
God sent His only Son from heaven above.
He took a beating for our healing; this we know is true.
And to cover all our sins, He hung from a cross too.
He healed, the sick, and blind and made the lame to walk.
People came from all over just to hear Him talk.
He forgave everyone's sins no matter what they had done,
And said, "If you're looking for the Messiah, I am the one."
The day He was risen, He beat death, hell, and the grave,
Now we can call on His name, and we can be saved.
If we want to go to heaven and walk streets of gold,
Just invite Him in your heart is what we've been told.
I will live and die believing every part of His Word,
Because as for me and my household, we will serve the Lord!

Give It Some Thought

God is pure love, full of mercy and of grace.
He is omnipresent, so He's in each and every place.
What better way to give praises to His name,
Then to shout hallelujah and glory all the same.
The righteous know the love and mercy of the Lord,
Not giving constant thanks daily we really can't afford.
If you want to see His miracles at hand,
Try fasting and praying, try taking a stand.
We see His mighty hand in many many ways,
His amazement never ceases throughout all our days.
Take a look around you and ponder in your mind,
How many beautiful things can you truly find?
Things we all know man could not make,
Raise your hands and praise Him, oh, for goodness' sake.
I will serve my Lord until the day that I die,
Because I can't wait to meet Him in the sky!

I Stand on His Word

I fast for their salvation in Jesus's name,
And He will be faithful in His own time frame.
He said raise them up in the way they should go,
And they will not depart, and I believe it is so.
I know that my Lord is just and true,
So I know what He says He will always do.
Satan, you have no power, and you are the father of lies,
So I stand on the Word of God because your ways I despise.
In the name of Jesus, you have no choice—you have to flee,
Because I'm tired of you in my church, and I'm tired of you in my family.
I'm going to defeat you as I take this stand,
Because I believe in the blood, and I'm a Holy Ghost-filled man.
Lord, I thank You now for my victory in this fight.
Your mercy and Your grace are always out of sight!

Renewal of Heart and Mind

What peace I find in the Lord up above.
I bask in His mercy, and I swim in His love.
The wonder of His grace is what I seek.
He offers it to His own when we are weak.
But never forget to give Him praise,
Because He is righteous in all His ways.
We cannot imagine the reason why,
Yet He still enjoys giving it by and by.
Never take for granted all of His gifts,
Especially the Holy Spirit, it truly uplifts.
Whenever you are lost just quote the Word,
Then believe that you receive no matter how absurd.
He never will fail you; I promise it's true.
He'll pick you up every time when you're feeling blue.
Yes, we all wonder how can this be.
Just try it out, and you will see.
Lift up your voice and holy hands,
Then make sure you follow all His commands.
Remember you're the head and not the tail,
So the cross and resurrection will never fail!

A Goal Worth Fighting For

Through fasting and prayer, you can reach your goal,
And also that helps to feed your soul.
While during this time, God plays His role,
So that in the end, your spirit is made whole.
In order to find the truth in your heart,
The Word of God is the place to start.
They say don't put the horse before the cart,
So if you come to Jesus, He will never depart.
God created the heavens and the earth too.
He created man from the dust; we know this is true.
He gave us His Word so we'd know what to do,
And He gave us free will, so it's purely up to you.
You may have lost the battle, but you can still win the war.
Put your faith in the Lord, and He will even up the score.
Endure to the end because God will open up the door.
Heaven is the goal we should be fighting for!

How to Have Happiness

Be slow to anger and quick to pray,
And things will get better every day.
Tame your tongue and guard what you say.
Let the Holy Spirit lead the way.
It's not a matter of what you can do,
Just let the love of God work through you.
Repent of your sins and daily renew,
Then give the Lord praise that He is due.
Laughter is always good for the soul,
And peace in your heart will make you whole.
To keep your foot on the rock and your name on the roll,
Keep your eyes on the cross, and to heaven, you will go.
We need to smile more and frown much less.
Don't get upset about this worldly mess.
It's the father of lies that we should address.
Resist that devil when our sins we confess!

I Long After Thee

Every time I think of You, my praises swell within me.
I always choose to honor You because the cross is what I see.
Keep Your hand upon me, Lord, this I always ask.
I long for Your grace. In Your mercy, I will bask.
The love that You show for each and every one
Never seems to change no matter what we've done.
I'm amazed at all Your ways, I have to admit.
All I have to do is search because Your path is always lit.
You supply all my strength in my time of need,
So I will always trust in You, and to Your Word, I'll heed.
To wrap Your loving arms around me every day,
And be the lamp unto my feet in Jesus's name, I pray!

Love from Above

If you will have faith the size of a mustard seed,
God will take care of anything that you need.
He can heal your mind, body, and soul.
Put your foot on the rock and your name on the roll.
Depression and pain, you'll have to flee,
In the name of Jesus, you will see.
Nothing is too hard for Him if you will believe.
Fervently pray, and you can receive.
I know it is hard to continue each day,
But I'll be your friend along the way.
I'll hold your hand and pray with you,
And when you have problems, I'll make them mine too.
I'll always be loyal all the way to the end.
God and I together will be your friend.
I will help you see His mercy and love,
And I promise you'll get your answer from above!

Make Jesus Your Path

When you come to a split in life's road,
Choose to ask God to carry this load.
Say, "Lord, should I go left or right?
I want to do what's good in Your sight."
Now read His Word and pray in the spirit,
Then wait on Him, and I promise He'll visit.
Listen to what He has to say,
Because He will always lead you the righteous way.
His promises are just and always true,
And He's already proven that He loves you.
Not one on this earth has a reason to doubt,
Because the cross showed us what His heart is about.
So when you need to know which path to take,
Remember Jesus is the choice that you should make!

A Christian Is Brave

If you say you are being brave,
To what your sinful nature does crave.
Say yes to God is what you should do,
Say yes to serving Him and righteousness too.
Remember to come to His throne and be bold,
And He will bless you with life is what we are told.
How could you ever possibly fail
When you are the head and not the tail?
You can't go to hell with gnashing of teeth
When you are above and not beneath.
The righteousness of Christ is who you are.
When it comes to love, He set the bar.
So don't ever worry and don't ever fear.
Be brave and believe God will always be near!

You Can't Afford to Give Up

No matter what, don't let go of your hope.
Hold on tight because He'll help you cope.
Grip tightly until your hands are sore.
Open your eyes and look for the door.
If you continue to ask, He'll show you the way.
Take all your burdens—in His hands, you should lay.
Hope is something you can't stand to lose.
Love and faith are what you should choose.
All of the pain and hurt that you feel,
Jesus can mend, and this is for real.
Stand, therefore, don't run and hide.
He is your friend, so in Jesus, confide!

The Answer Is Plain

I know you have questions if you'll get by.
We all have days that we wonder why.
Not a day goes by without God's unfolding grace.
Just look around you, He's all over the place.
He's in the face of your children or in the heart of a friend.
Get on your knees, and His mercy, He'll send.
True peace and happiness you can find every day.
Look in His Word, and He'll show you the way.
To be a productive part of mankind,
Look in your heart and see what you find.
God has a work that He wants us to do,
And He has a plan for me and for you.
Pray in the spirit, and you will know,
The plan for your life, God will show!

Fear Not, He's with You

Anytime you have a mountain of fear,
Look to the Lord, and the answer will be clear.
He'll give you joy while He brings you peace.
His love and His grace, He will release.
According to His Word, there is no doubt.
Trusting in Him is what it's all about.
Every day more, I love this path I chose,
To follow Jesus because He always knows.
Exactly what we all need.
If His commands, we will heed.
Never look to the left or right,
And don't give up without a fight.
Stand, therefore, and He'll be there.
Then you will meet Him in the air!

The Wave of Our Savior

The angel told the women, "Jesus ain't here.
Now go tell the others and don't worry—don't fear.
Tell them that Jesus will be in Galilee.
Gather yourselves together, and you will see
His nail-scarred hands and His pierced side.
Believe in Him, and with the Father, you will abide."
He said, "The one who comes after Me is the Comforter for you,
To help you to live righteous and also to live true."
He will give you power to overcome evil ways
And also give you strength to withstand these evil days.
Yes, on this earth, the devil, he does roam.
But as long as you resist him, you will have a heavenly home.
That is the story of how Jesus beat the grave,
And then sent His spirit to give us a mighty spiritual wave!

My Cry of Enjoyment

With a humble heart, I cry out to my friend,
"You'll be my Lord all the way to the end.
I turn my life completely over to You,
And now I can't wait to see what You'll do.
You're healing miracles are what You're known for,
And I wait for you to walk me out this jail door.
Get Shirley and I married at last,
And heal her body just as fast.
Give my mom and my grandmother strength to stand,
Then allow me to lend the poor a helping hand.
I want to go to Bible college and get a degree,
Learn Your way in the music ministry.
I will use it to lead others to the cross
And proclaim to the world that You are the Boss!"

It's Deeper Than You Think

There is a peace from God above,
That shows His compassion and His love.
It can be perfect if you trust in the Lord.
True understanding comes from His Word.
It says He'll guard your heart and your mind,
Only a blessing of the Jesus kind.
He also gives His people strength.
To get this from Him, I'll go to any length.
Isaiah said, "Our Lord is the Prince of Peace.
If you depend on Him, He will meet your needs."
It is the evidence of the Holy Spirit's work.
You need this peace because depression does lurk.
Let it saturate your mind and your soul,
Knowing that you're saved and your name is on the roll!

Everything's Gonna Be Alright

The Lord says fear not for He is with you.
Be anxious for nothing that you set out to do.
They say we have nothing to fear but fear itself,
They also say don't put love up on no shelf.
I believe that fear and love are connected to one another,
Because Paul said if you have a problem, you should turn to your brother.
It's also said that love covers a multitude of sins,
And fear is just an evil of the devil within.
So if the love of God is in us; there's no room for fear.
Just remember we're children of God, and He considers us dear.
You have no reason to worry if you think about what I say.
As long as you're a Christian, you're going to heaven one day!

Know That He's in Charge

Think about what you do and also what you say,
When you consider both these things, are they the Jesus's way?
The meaning of the phrase, *What would Jesus do?*
Is that in your whole life make sure that He's with you.
Jesus said, "Put everything aside and follow Me.
Trust in the Father and you'll have the victory."
What you put into, this is what you'll get out.
So when you overcome, praise Him with a shout.
I give you the truth in the words of the Lord.
To defeat the devil, you should use the sword.
Quote the Word of God is what this does mean,
That's when you put God directly on the scene!

A True Christian Walk

If you put your trust in God in the face of your fear,
You will find peace, and to His heart, you'll draw near.
These are facts that I know not just what I've heard,
Because these are the promises that are written in His Word.
Sharing His truth with others brings me joy that is great.
I think God for salvation before it was too late.
I'm finally out of darkness because I walk in His light.
He feels me, full of hope, and helps me do what's right.
Because of free will, the choice is yours—that is true.
You either serve God or Satan; it is clearly up to you.
When you walk the fence and you're confused, you wonder why,
It's because there is no third choice—don't believe that vicious lie.
I'm so thankful that Jesus showed me the right choice.
Now one day, I'll be in heaven, and forever I'll rejoice!

How Great Is God

If we are not sure, His Word makes it clear.
For those who are deaf, He helps them to hear.
He says, "I'm the way, the truth, and the light."
For those who are blind, He gives them their sight.
In the Bible, we can hear God talk.
For those who are lame, He helps them walk.
There are so many miracles that He will do,
But the greatest is salvation for me and for you.
When Jesus came to earth, the way had been made,
And when He died on the cross, the price had been paid.
To accept His blessings, all we have to do is come.
This offer is to all not just for some!

Be His Mirror Image

With all the things to do from day to day,
We should take a moment to see what Jesus has to say.
We get so busy as we go from place to place,
That we forget our daily purpose should be to seek His face.
Get on our knees and raise holy hands.
Pray to the Lord and see where He stands.
Are we doing what we should to bring glory to His name?
Jesus came to serve and said we should do the same.
He said, "Love one another as I love you all,"
And being Christlike is the true Christian call.
Don't let pride say it's about you.
We should show Jesus in what we say and what we do.
Because He died for our sins that day upon the cross,
We should show His love to all who are lost!

Give It to the Lord

To have victory in the battle of our mind and soul,
A closeness to our Lord should be our goal.
By prayer and the Word, we can be free.
The love of Christ in us is what others should see.
The Bible says faith without works is dead,
So to have true peace, we should be Spirit-led.
You don't have to worry; everything will be fine.
Going through trials shows His glory is divine.
We need to remember that Satan is real,
And his purpose is to steal, destroy, and kill.
The battle won't end, but you can help it to ease.
Just honor the Lord, and He will bring you peace!

I Want to Be an Example of Jesus

Walking in His spirit is where I always want to be.
And one day, the face of God is what I really want to see.
Every day I strive to live a life that is right,
And I want to keep my heart pure in His sight.
When you look at me, can you see our Lord?
Do I show all the love into me He has poured?
All day I pray that God shows me when I do wrong,
Because I know when we are weak, the Lord can make us strong.
As long as we believe that Jesus is the only way,
He will guide our steps each and every day.
Do I shine the light of Christ? I ask to each of you,
Because I want to help others find Jesus too.
My number one goal is to show you all true love,
Because that's the top command from the One up above!

It's Simple, Just Choose

Service and worship make a balanced Christian walk,
And to not be a hypocrite, you have to practice what you talk.
Love the Lord with all your heart, soul, strength, and mind,
And love your neighbor as yourself will show you are kind.
Raise holy hands to God and praise Him all day long,
And be there for your brother to help him stay strong.
This is how we know that Jesus is our Lord.
Others will see that we live by the sword.
I'm speaking of the Bible; it helps everyone.
And when Jesus paid the price, He said, "It is done."
Don't try to make excuses, just do what is right.
Tell others about salvation and walk in His light.
It's all very simple to follow God's call,
Just ask for forgiveness, and He'll pick you up when you fall!

The Ultimate Shield

I fight this depression every day.
I pray that the Lord will show me the way.
The Word says the darkness is overpowered by light,
So I give it to God for Him to fight.
He can bring peace from the inside out.
We must claim the victory and do not doubt.
I know that it is hard to battle the mind,
But through Jesus Christ, deliverance you can find.
Put on the helmet of salvation to start,
And the breastplate of righteousness to protect your heart.
Make sure that you daily repent of your sins.
This is a battle that with God, you can win.
He is our complete protection from all,
And He'll be by your side whenever you call!

Live Each Day the Jesus Way

God will convict your stubborn heart.
That is where this walk with Jesus does start.
God places extra in front of ordinary for you and I,
Like He so marvelously placed the stars in the sky.
For all of us, the path to heaven has been paved,
When Jesus died on the cross so we could be saved.
He took stripes on His back so we could be healed,
And when He rose from the grave, Satan's fate was sealed.
He takes the dull in our life and makes it divine,
Puts joy in the hearts of yours and of mine.
He makes no mistakes and knows exactly what to do,
And He showed the ultimate love for me and for you.
Give Him all praise glory and honor each day,
And share with the world that Jesus is the way.

Let Me Shoot It Straight

The Lord gives us strength, and He fills us with His love.
But remember we can do nothing without the One up above.
When we ask for His help, we must believe it is true.
Stand on His promises because that's exactly what He'll do.
Memorize the Word and quote it every day.
Then let Jesus Christ guide you on your way.
Don't let Satan remind you of your past.
A reminder of the blood will shut him up real fast.
Look in your heart each day and search that it is pure.
Don't take any chances; repent each night to be sure.
I say these things to you so we can help each other not to fail,
To sin on purpose is a one-way ticket straight to hell!

One Honest Kiss for Heavenly Bliss

I know that our relationship is meant from above.
And from the very start, you've had my heartfelt love.
Now I know I messed up, and I've done you wrong,
It's brought me to my knees, and I thought about it long.
Remember I'm just me a simple man,
But the One up above gave me a better plan.
I ask for His forgiveness and yours too,
And with guidance from Him, I'll be a better man to you.
So give me a chance, and I'll show you it's not just talk.
When I get out of here, I'll continue this walk.
The Word of God is showing me a better way.
And from here on out, I'll practice what I say.
I'm a changed man, and my word is my bond.
So remember that I love you to infinity and beyond!

1 Corinthians 13:4–8, 13
Ephesians 3:20; 4:2
Philippians 4:13

Let Me Tell You Something Good

Knowing where we come from and knowing where we're going,
It's part of growing up, and as Christians, we are showing.
We are all born sinners and saved by His grace,
And in the end, what we want is to see His face.
So if we strive to stay holy and obey His every command,
Then on Judgment Day before Him blameless we can stand.
What a wonderful day in heaven that will be,
When He says, "My good and faithful servant, come and sit with Me."
I don't know about you, but I will dance with all my might,
Because no longer all these sins will I ever have to fight.
I can't wait to walk the streets of gold,
While I shout glory and His nail-scarred hand I hold.
Thinking about all this makes it easier to persevere,
And He gave us His holy word to show us how to adhere.
To make this happen, you have to ask Him in your heart,
But you must believe that He is God from the very start!

Let Me Make It Clear

You should ask Him in what are you waiting for.
He stands at your heart, knocking at the door.
You need to realize it doesn't matter what you've done,
Who can forgive you? He is the One.
Just repent of your sins and walk the other way.
Read His holy word each and every day.
It's really that simple; you should give Him a try.
My life is full of joy, and He's the reason why.
Believe He died on the cross and rose from the grave,
And He did all this for you and I to save.
When you have a problem, with Jesus you can lean,
And the sight of heaven will be the most beautiful scene.
I want to serve God from now until the end,
If for no other reason than Jesus is my best friend!

One Way Is the Right Way

I pray every day that I follow God's call,
So that when I stand before Him, I can stand tall.
I know I will stumble, but I don't want to fail.
Let everyone know I have a story to tell.
A story of Jesus who died on the cross,
For you and for me and all of the lost.
Faith in Christ is what you need.
Read the Word of God and follow His lead.
Jesus is the only way to choose,
Any other path and you will lose.
If you want to be sure you are heaven-bound,
Forgiveness through Christ is the only way it can be found.
You don't have to worry—He loves everyone.
He gave up His life and said, "It is done."
He took stripes on His back so we could be healed,
And when He rose from the grave, Satan's fate was sealed.
So now every minute and every hour, I pray,
Let me shine the light of God every day!

He's a No-Worries Mate

Jesus was God who became a man.
He was and always will be your biggest fan.
He is what you'd call a sacred delight.
With Him, you're guaranteed to win every fight.
He stands at the door of everyone's heart
And fills us with joy from the very start.
He's your Father, your Lawyer, and your Best Friend.
He'll be the most loyal from beginning to end.
Put your trust in Him because He never will fail,
And He's the only One who can save you from hell.
Get on your knees and repent of your sin.
Pray to the Lord and invite Him in.
You no longer have to worry about your past.
You may still have troubles, but they won't last.
He will deliver you and heal you too.
You can rest assured that God cheers for you!

The Keys to the Kingdom

Jesus makes promises in the Sermon on the Mount,
Eight to be exact if you're keeping count.
Most of these He made to the average Joe,
With no further ado, I'm going to tell you how they go.
The poor in spirit to the beggars on the street,
Those who mourn is every sinner that you meet.
The meek have God-given talents that no one even knows.
Those who hunger and thirst know right from wrong, and it shows.
The merciful you'll find will share anything.
The pure in heart always have a song to sing.
The peacemakers are repairers of the breach.
While the persecuted no matter what God they teach.
God's final promise—oh yeah, that makes nine.
He said, "Be like these, and heaven is yours and Mine!"

From the Valley to the Summit

He gives a joy you can't quench and a peace you can't steal.
There's no problem He can't solve and no sickness He can't heal.
God gives a radical reconstruction of the heart,
A complete change of attitude, not just part.
God's holy joy is within your reach.
You are just one decision away is what His Word does teach.
God can work a miracle; it doesn't matter who you are.
Just look at all the prophets in the Bible He's used so far.
Noah, Abraham, Isaac, Jacob, Joseph, Moses too,
The blessings of these six men should encourage me and you.
Pull up a chair and talk to your friend.
It's as simple as that; the prayers you can send.
Ask Jesus to sit and have a good talk,
And He'll take you to the mountain, and with you, He will walk!

I Seek Applause from Heaven

Doing my time in Coffee County jail,
Leading others to Christ so they don't go to hell.
I don't know why I've been here so long,
But it's not going to stop me from singing God's song.
What song do you ask—let me give you a clue.
My heart gets made pure doing what God says to do.
I've repented of my sins and walked the other way.
I have fellowship with Jesus each and every day.
Walking the straight and narrow in here is no easy task.
I pray to God daily, and here is what I ask.
I don't ask for special treatment or to be the boss of the pod,
No to fame and fortune, just a closer walk with God.
It's all very simple if you think about it clear.
The more you please Him, heaven draws ever near.
So I'll make it short and sweet; peace will suffice.
I'm on the winning team, and my coach is Jesus Christ!

From My Heart

Are you worried about your future? Are you worried about mine?
I will pray God give you wisdom, and I assure you I am fine.
I don't say that with conceit, but I tell you it's true,
Because I've accepted Jesus Christ, and He tells me what to do.
I've asked Him for forgiveness and read His Word every day,
And when I need guidance, to God only do I pray.
He gives me understanding of how I need to act,
And I know I'm okay because He and I have made a pact.
He promised I'd go to heaven if I believed in His Son,
And I made a lifetime promise He'd be the only one.
I will never turn my back because my word is my bond.
He might not answer when I want, but He always does respond.
Not always does He do what we think He should,
But I know what He does is for our own good.
I pray He gives me faith and strength to endure.
He'll supply all my needs—of that I am sure.
He's the Alpha and Omega, the beginning and the end,
He's my ever-loving Father, my most loyal, true best friend!

This Is My Utmost Desire

Jesus has given me a reason to fight.
That's why I want to worship Him with all of my might.
Dance before the Lord and sing and shout.
Thank Him for putting me on the right route.
Release me from this place, God, so I can go to church.
Every time the doors are open and continue my search.
To get closer to God than ever before,
I have fellowship with Jesus, but I want more.
More of His joy and more of His peace,
More of His love that will never cease.
Every day that goes by, I know heaven is close,
But to see the Master's face is what I want most!

Find Life in Truth

Take a look deep in your heart
And ask the Master where you need to start.
To switch your path and change your ways,
To serve the Lord through all your days.
If you don't want to receive God's wrath,
Just ask Him honestly, and He'll guide your path.
Look to the cross and ask Jesus to come in.
Ask for forgiveness, and He'll wash away your sin.
Turn your life around before it's too late.
There's joy in the Lord, so why would you wait?
There's peace in God that's beyond all measure.
If you ask, "Will You help me?", He'll say, "My pleasure."
The greatest thing you'll find is His unending love,
And the fact in the end you go to heaven above.
Don't wait until later; accept Him today.
To get to heaven, there is no other way!

God-Given Joy and Peace

No matter what your problem, God can solve anything.
Make sure when He does, His praises you to sing.
God has a timing that is not like our own,
But through all the ages His faithfulness has shown.
I think when I was born, the one who gave me life,
She not only raised me up but also has been there during strife.
He gave me a mother who is a true gem,
But that's not the only way He showed I'm blessed by Him.
He's now blessed me with a woman who is a lot like her.
That's why I know that Shirley will stay with me for sure.
The greatest part about it is they get along,
And I sit back and listen to them sing the same song.
I'm the one important in both of their hearts.
The three of us have a bond that no one will tear apart.
I called these two women my joy and my peace,
And the loyalty and love I have for them will never cease!

Standing on Your Promises

Lord, I'm only asking You to do what You say You will.
I'm seeking You wholeheartedly, but I'm in captivity still.
I don't care about the fortunes; send me back to where I came.
I've been telling about You to others, and I'll continue to do the same.
I haven't given up on You, so why have You given up on me?
I encourage everyone around me, and Your promises, I expect to see.
You say the quote Your Word and daily on Your promises, I should stand,
Well, that's what I'm doing, so bring me back to my homeland.
How can those I preach to believe what I say is true,
If You won't even do for me what You say that You will do.
For Moses, you talk through a bush and parted the Red Sea,
But You won't even keep one promise that I'm asking for me.
For almost two straight years, I've been bearing my cross,
Leading others to You, who are dying and lost.
Take me home, Lord, on the straight and narrow I have stayed.
All I'm asking from You is to keep the promise that You made!

This Ain't No Game

Now I'm getting down to the grit of how I feel.
I don't know how to be fake because I know that You are real.
I want to believe that Your promises are true.
All the things that You've said, I'm waiting for You to do.
My heart is growing weary, but I'm trying to stay strong.
I stand on Your Word because I think none of it is wrong.
I just need a little hint that going home is near.
Don't beat around the bush; make it perfectly clear.
I know You talk to us all each and our own way,
When am I going home, Lord, I'm waiting for You to say.
I serve only You, Lord, with my whole heart,
So take my whole life each and every part!

Wake Up, It's Time

Lord, our hearts and souls and spirits are broken before You.
We know that we are hurting, yet some do not know what to do.
Lead and guide those of us who know what Your Word does command,
Comfort the brokenhearted and show that on the solid rock, we should stand.
In times of crisis and tragedy, it's hard to do what we say.
Lord, help me be a lighthouse of comfort to those in pain today.
I have to get past my own arrogance and hurtful needs
To make sure that Your agenda and glory is what supersedes.
I don't want to get in the way of where You've called me to be,
And when others look at my life, the love of Christ is what I want them to see.
Lord, stay by my side because I know I'll falter and fail,
So when I have victory, I'll have a story to tell.
It's a story of when I was weak, someone helped me to be strong.
That someone is Jesus Christ, and with Him, you can't go wrong!

Do Not Doubt and You Will Shout

Thank God for answered prayers.
He says He's numbered all our hairs.
I asked to be removed from the hole,
And that's exactly what He did show.
He always does what we ask Him to do,
And usually with a little extra too.
Exceeding abundantly above all we ask or think,
And deep in our hearts does His love sink.
So I gave Him glory and honor and praise,
Holy hands to Him I raise.
On my knees and my face is where I should be,
Total obedience is what He wants to see.
My Lord is good to me every day.
I tell everyone that Jesus is the only way.
I can't wait to see what He has for me next.
Going home is what I expect.
Whatever you want, you have to believe.
Trust in God, and you will receive!

I'm So Excited

I dance before God because I'm thrilled.
This is what happens when you're Spirit-filled.
You pray in tongues, and you shout.
You run the aisles, and you sing out loud.
Being baptized in the Spirit is really cool.
That's when you know in your life, God does rule.
I want to share His message with everyone,
To go to heaven, accept His Son.
Go to the cross for forgiveness of sins,
And feel the Holy Spirit rise within.
God will change you from the inside out,
And Jesus showed us what love is about.
Spread His Word and follow His way,
Then your life will have joy and peace today.
To remove your past and have a new start,
Ask Jesus Christ into your heart!

Don't Retreat, God Will Defeat

Do you believe in love? Do you believe in peace?
Do you believe forgiveness is what the Father can release?
Do you believe contentment is what we all can find?
Do you believe as Christians, we should all be kind?
Those who harm His children will receive a curse.
It's written in the Bible; I can show you chapter and verse.
You do not have to live in hiding and fear,
Those who are evil will always be made clear.
Just because you're a Christian doesn't mean you have to run.
Do you believe in Jesus, He's the Almighty Son?
When you go to the cross, He forgives all your sins.
God believes in battle, and believe me, He wins!

It's Time for Battle

Let's get ready for what we have to do
This is a battle both for me and for you.
First, you must be strong in the Lord,
If you plan to fight Satan's unholy horde.
Belt of truth so you know where you stand,
Breastplate of righteousness to fight the evil at hand,
Shoes of peace to show God is love,
Shield of faith knowing it all comes from above.
Helmet of salvation teaching Jesus is the way,
Sword of the Spirit, stay in His Word every day.
Pray in the Spirit every day and every hour,
With all of this armor, He'll give you the power.
It's not against people but Satan that we fight,
But the Father Son and Holy Ghost is out of sight!

What It's All About

Love is patient, and love is kind.
With love, there's no jealousy in the mind.
Love is not boastful nor is it proud,
Rudeness and irritability are not allowed.
Love does not demand its own way.
A record of being wronged, it will never say.
Love doesn't rejoice about injustice, only when truth wins out.
It never gives up or loses faith; there is no doubt.
Love is always hopeful and endures through everything.
Love will last forever, and it will make your heart sing.
Three things will last forever—faith, hope, and love,
But love is the greatest like Jesus up above!

1 Corinthians 13:4–7, 13

Keeping It Real

Though we live in a world full of hate and fear,
My generosity and love for others have been made perfectly clear.
I try to show Jesus in everything that I do,
And that the walk in my life has been made brand-new.
Everyone I speak to I tell them Jesus is the way,
And I present the love of Christ in everything that I say.
How can we say that we're a Christian to everyone,
If they can't look at our life and see what He has done?
God will change you from the inside out.
Leading others to Him is what being a Christian is about.
If you don't practice what you preach, it doesn't matter at all.
So, Lord, help me be pure and holy so I don't make others fall.
In the presence of the Lord is where I want to be,
And God in my heart is what I hope others will see!

Set the Standard

Can you expect to go to heaven if you don't keep His command?
Can you expect to go to heaven if for Jesus, you won't stand?
If you deny Him before others, He'll deny you too.
But why would you want to miss out on what He has for you?
We need to take this seriously because serving Christ is real.
Don't be ashamed; let Him know how you feel.
How in love you are with Jesus everyone should see,
Baptized in the Spirit is what I always want to be.
Don't play with God; being holy ain't a game,
No matter who you are, He loves us all the same.
Come to the cross and show you love the Lord.
Learn to forgive and live by the sword.
Lean on the power from God up above.
Be holy and audacious in the Father's love!

Put Family Before Friends

Family is important to the Lord up above.
It's one of the things He mentions when He talks about love.
If you don't care for your relatives, you've denied the faith—that's true.
You're worse than unbelievers, and that's not what you want to do.
How important to God is your own blood?
That's the only people He told Noah to take and hide from the flood.
He told Cain when he killed Abel, "His blood cries out to Me."
Now you are cursed and banished, so it's important as you see.
He gave Moses his brother, Aaron, to help him to speak.
Family morals and values are what we all should seek.
John was Jesus's brother, and He loved him He did say,
And God gave His only Son, so loving family is the way!

It's Bubbling in My Soul

If you don't turn from the way you were, you'll remain where you're at.
You have to accept Christ in your heart no matter what, and that is that.
Three things I know for certain—I am saved, and I am filled.
That's with the Holy Spirit, so the third is I am thrilled.
I am not ashamed of the Gospel that I know,
And until the day that I die, I will let it show.
The joy of the Lord is never dull or mundane,
And the wisdom that He gives is uplifting and profane.
You can experience everything that I've said.
Just believe Jesus died on the cross and was raised from the dead.
Living for God, I know now is the only way,
And I don't know when, but I'm going to heaven one day!

It's a Wonderful Life

He looked down from heaven and brought peace to my soul,
And He took a beating so my body would be whole.
He repairs my beaten life and shows that He is real.
No matter what I'm going through, He always knows how I feel.
No matter where we're at, He's there for you and me.
We must be sincere because our heart is what He'll see.
He died on the cross for me and for you.
He forgives all our sins, and that's what He'll continue to do.
Say the Word out loud because Satan can't read your thoughts,
So I talk about my love for Jesus, and I say it a lot.
I don't care what others think, and I'm not putting on a show.
I'm not here to please man; Heaven is where I want to go!

Let's Get Together

Do you know Jesus? Would you like to today?
I can tell you about Him; I can show you the way.
Have you read the Bible? Do you know what Jesus said?
I can read it to you; His words are written in red.
Have you ever felt true peace or joy from within?
Let me tell you about a Savior who can remove all your sins.
Do you wonder where you're going, or why you're even here?
If you give your heart to Jesus, He'll make it perfectly clear.
Choose to walk with God and do what is right.
Let Him lead you out of darkness and into the light.
He will heal your body and also save your soul,
If you give up this life and make following Jesus your goal!

Take Up Your Cross and Follow

When it comes to Jesus, where do you stand?
Joy and salvation—they go hand in hand.
God gives a challenge to me and to you.
He says, "There's free will. Now what will you do?"
Will you show the love of Christ to each and every one?
Will you go to your friends and tell what God has done?
Don't be ashamed of what the Lord represents.
Go to the cross, and your sins, you should repent.
Repent means you're sorry and you turn the other way.
Don't do what you've been doing, not another day.
If you are serious and heaven is where you want to go,
The way you live your life will absolutely show.
Do you want to be a Christian? I don't know how you feel,
But whichever side you choose, you better keep it REAL!

Here's a Reality Check

If you promote others to sin,
You are evil from deep within.
Because you know what is right,
And yet you don't put up a fight.
So if you are ashamed of the Lord,
You'll be judged by the sword
Because God is true and just,
Being righteous and faithful, you must.
It's really not that hard to do,
Depends on what's important to you.
Your life will show how you really feel,
Because your heart will keep it REAL,
What's in your heart, your mouth will say,
So believe that Jesus is the only way.
I hope that I have made my point.
Let's lift God up in this joint!

Can You Feel That?

The Bible says to have the faith of a mustard seed.
That's how you'll get whatever you need.
Go to the Father and ask with a pure heart,
And you must believe right from the very start.
Believe what you ask in faith, and He will do.
There's power in the blood both for me and for you.
He heals sickness and disease and frees us from all our sins,
Mends the brokenhearted and cleans our life from within.
He gives us free will; it's your choice to believe.
It's the greatest gift that I ever did receive.
There's only one source, and that is God up above.
Come and feel the power of His almighty love!

Let Him Shine on You

We all go through different phases all throughout our years.
We deal with these phases like we deal with our fears.
At first, we try to hide them so no one can tell.
No matter how you cover up, this will always fail.
Because when you try to put something out of sight,
That's the first thing that will show in the light.
The Bible teaches what you do in secret always shows.
Man may not see it, but God always knows.
If you read the Word of God, here's what you'll find,
Pray to God and believe, and He'll move them from your mind.
That's when I tell the devil he's trespassing on holy ground,
Because where I walk today, Jesus can be found!

Learn to Fly So You Don't Fall

"Soar high on wings like eagles," said Isaiah the Saint.
You will run and not grow weary, walk and not faint.
Jesus said He'll carry you whenever you are feeling weak.
You can accomplish anything as long as it's the Lord you seek.
Trust in the Lord because He knows your ins and outs,
He'll pick you up when you fall and remove all your doubts.
If you walk hand in hand with God and abide in His love,
You're bound to fly high since He resides in the sky above.
It may seem real silly when you think about it all,
But positive thinking is what you need to heed unto His call.
If we stay devoted to Jesus, He says we'll fly in the end,
Because we'll meet Him in the sky, and we'll never fall again.

Holy Ghost Grind

Do you choose God or Satan? Do you choose heaven or hell?
Soon you'll run out of time, and all I can say is, "Oh well."
I may sound like a broken record repeating myself every day,
But everything I'm telling you are things that I have to say.
You need to know that we are getting close to the end of time,
So everyone really should listen to my Holy Ghost rhyme.
You need to trust in God and lean not to your own understanding,
Accept Jesus and read your Bible so that you know what He's planning.
You shouldn't serve yourself—don't believe that lie.
If you wonder why I keep repeating myself, it's because I love you, and hell is real—that's why.
If you want to know what you need to do when your back is against the wall,
Accept Jesus as your Savior, turn your life around, and make God your all in all!

It's Okay to Admit It

Imagine for a moment the death and pain that's all around.
Now think about the love of Christ that could be found.
Look at your mistakes that you need to confess.
Look at your life and how you've made it a mess.
We all need a Savior each and every one.
We need to ask for forgiveness for the wrongs we have done.
None of us are perfect at least not right now.
But one day, we can be, and I can tell you how.
Accept Jesus in your heart and turn from your evil way.
Follow God and believe you'll live in heaven one day.
Giving Satan a black eye is a much more righteous fight,
So love your fellow humans and lead them to the light.
Help your brother up when they're down or they fall,
That's what being a Christian is about after all!

You Are Worth It

To be Christlike, what should you do?
You should love one another as He loves you.
Love is unconditional; we know this for sure.
He always thinks about His children, and His thoughts are always pure.
So don't let the devil lie to your mind.
Each one of us is special, a one-of-a-kind.
There is not another like you, no, not one.
God said, "Look at the masterpiece that I have done."
He makes no mistakes; you are perfect in His eyes,
So quit believing all the devil's evil lies.
So who we are in Jesus, we can be proud.
That's the only kind of pride that we are allowed.
Share the joy and love of Jesus with everyone today,
Because forgiveness through Christ is the only way!

My Thoughts Voiced

I write of sound spirit but not of sound mind.
I know Jesus saves, but am I His kind?
Do I have what it takes to be accepted by the Lord?
I search for a clue written on the sword.
I try to find where it says, "Wyatt, you're okay."
I just wonder if I really make a difference today.
Would anyone care if I were to die?
Have I shown the love of Christ who reigns up on high?
Has a single person changed by something I may have said?
Have I impressed on the world the words written in red?
I'm really concerned because I know my time is near.
I hope the love of Jesus is what I've made clear.
I have to believe that my sins He did erase,
Because I know that I'm about to see God's face!

A Soldier's Fatigue

They are breaking down my spirit, literally breaking it into.
What is a spiritual man supposed to do?
I pray to the Lord and believe for His touch.
I expected persecution but not quite this much.
They are destroying my body both outside and in.
My patience for these people is wearing so thin.
I don't know how much longer I can hide my pain.
Soon they're going to see that I'm going insane.
What will happen once they fracture my mind?
They may no longer like the me that they find.
Lord, I'm begging You to remove me from this place,
Before what's left of my heart is lost without a trace.
I'm trying to keep all this hatred out of sight,
But I'm getting so tired and asking You to fight!

Be a Real Leader

I sit normally; all the things that race through my mind,
Like is it okay to be so generous or continuously be kind,
Helping others to be better day after day,
Showing them the path to a better way?
I know it can be dangerous, but I don't care.
I just want everyone to have a home in the air.
Showing others the love of Jesus—that is my goal.
I don't think about the risks, just that their name is on the roll.
Make God number one, and you'll see what I mean.
Love will permeate your mind when the Holy Spirit is on the scene.
Jesus heals the sick, and He saves the lost.
All we have to do is lead them to the cross!

It's Okay to Be a Jesus Freak

I don't care about being odd or weird at all,
For us to be peculiar—that is our call.
If being closer to God is what we seek,
Then I pray that I'm considered a Jesus freak.
Keep it one hundred because 99 percent just won't do.
He only wants what is best for me and for you.
So why not give your whole life to the Lord,
And do whatever it takes to live by the sword.
Stop all these labels we put on each other.
Put Jesus first and love your brother.
So being a Jesus freak is really okay,
As long as we all go to heaven one day!

It's Really Not That Hard

Do you understand what it means to be a Christian?
Do you understand what it means to be REAL?
Do you understand what it means to truly listen?
Do you understand what it means to truly feel?
Do you understand what it means to forgive?
Do you understand what it means to really love?
Do you understand what God gave for us to live?
Do you understand what awaits us up above?
Do you understand what it means to repent?
Do you understand that Jesus died upon the cross?
Do you understand what the Savior meant?
Do you understand that everyone is lost?
Do you understand?
Jesus is the Master Plan!

You Can't Hide

Feelings are something we all have, and they're within our control.
Keeping them on a positive note should be our daily goal.
How you feel about others will expose your Christian walk.
And how you live your life is REAL, not how you talk.
When you give your heart to Jesus, nothing will be the same.
Everyone will notice because everything will change.
The first thing they'll see in you is joy and peace within.
Then God will bring you conviction to do no wrong again.
As you pray and read His Word, He'll be your guiding light.
And when the devil attacks you, God will help you fight.
He showed what it means to love when He sent His only Son,
Who died upon a cross for the sins of everyone.
So if you say that you're a Christian, others will watch how you act,
And if you truly serve the Lord, it will show, and that's a fact!

The Truth Will Set You Free

If you want to know if someone's faithful and what they say is true,
Just give it time and watch what they do.
As the days go by, their true colors show.
They will show what's in their heart, and then you will know.
Then you'll know if they're fake because not everyone is REAL.
What I'm saying may not be popular, but it is how I feel.
The truth is what I preach each and every day,
And Jesus is who I serve because He is the only way.
I'm in the army of the Lord, and I'm loyal to the Son.
And I follow the commands of God each and every one.
Being a true Christian is what means the most to me.
The truth and love of Jesus is what I want others to see.
I have to be honest; the truth will bring release.
It will open your heart and bring joy and peace!

We Represent the Meaning of the Word

We all look at Christianity a different way,
But what really matters is what Jesus has to say.
We shouldn't interpret it the way we want,
Because the Word of God is final and very upfront.
If you allow the Holy Spirit to overtake your soul,
Wisdom and knowledge will become your goal.
That's when God will show you what's right,
And the Bible will become your guiding light.
You will no longer see it the way that you think,
Instead, you will notice a special link.
A link to the heavens and into God's mind,
Which leads you to be the Christlike kind.
You'll act differently from what you did before,
And your life will present a heavenly door.
To be an example of what the Bible does mean,
To lead others to Christ so their hearts are clean!

He Is the Master, There Is No Doubt

Have you noticed how a deer leaps as pretty as you please?
Have you noticed the perfect flow of the rivers or the trees?
Have you noticed the beauty of a rainbow in the sky?
Have you noticed how the sun sets and sat and wondered why?
Have you noticed how a child's love is sincere?
Or how the love of a mother can remove all your fear?
When you think of these things, you should know God is real.
He knows what you need, and He knows how you feel.
If you put your trust in Him on the solid rock, you'll stand.
When you stumble and you fall, let Him take you by the hand.
He makes no mistakes and is perfect in all His ways.
Make Him the Lord of your life and give Him all the praise.
Just take a look around at all the beauty He has shown.
That proves He is King of kings, and He is God alone!

Show What's Important to You

Look into your heart, deep into your soul,
What does it say about you? What does it show?
Are you full of love or evil to the core?
When you think of life and death, what do you want more?
When you look at the world, do you see the good in everyone?
When you look at your life, are you ashamed of what you've done?
Have you asked Jesus Christ to come into your heart?
Have you made a commitment to make a new start?
Do you know what the Bible instructs you to do?
Did you know that Jesus died on the cross just for you?
Remember God is faithful in all of His ways.
So raise only hands and give Him all of the praise!

There's Joy in Our Praise

I shout for joy within my soul. I praise His holy name.
I know that things are looking dim, yet I exalt Him all the same.
I worship God with all my heart for all His wonderful ways,
And I will continue to love the Lord throughout all my days.
Nothing could make me turn on Him never ever again,
Because I know that He watched over me through all my awful sins.
Lord, I thank You for the cross that saved a wretch like me.
I praise You for Your mercy and grace and how You've set me free.
Lord, You are the greatest, and of that, I have no doubts.
And You have lifted me higher than the eagles in the clouds.
Jesus is the answer, and this I claim is true.
The joy and peace He's given me, He will also give to you.
All you have to do is ask Him into your heart.
You just have to come to Him because He was there from the start!

Beating Down the Doors of Hell

Are you living for the Lord today? Are you walking in the light?
Do you know that is the only way to be righteous in His sight?
Do you have the love of Jesus planted in your heart?
Accepting Him as your Savior is where you need to start.
Take everything that you've done wrong, and to Him, you must confess.
And He will cast away all your sins as far as the east is to the west.
Ask for the baptism of the Holy Ghost is the next thing you should do,
Because the power and joy that will fill your life is, oh, so very cool.
They may call me a fanatic or weird, but I don't really care.
I will have the last laugh when I meet Him in the air.
We all will have ups and downs; that is a well-known fact.
But a Spirit-filled Christian has victory when we're attacked.
This is not just something I've heard; I live it every day.
The demons of hell better beware—and, Satan, get out of my way.
I am on a mission, and I've been sent by the Lord.
I'm gonna destroy you by my testimony and the sword!

Realizing Heaven as Home

I may have never been to heaven, but I know one day I will.
And I may not know exactly what it's like, but I know it will be a thrill.
A river of life will flow down streets of gold.
We'll have new heavenly bodies and be done with the old.
We will share in God's glory, and life will be complete.
No more sadness or pain; no more evil in the street.
God will be our focus, and Jesus will take us there.
There will be no more darkness and only righteousness in the air.
Walls of sapphire, emerald, and gates made of pearl.
We will walk with our Lord in this new and beautiful world.
Narrow is the road, yet Jesus is the way.
We are to think about heaven each and every day.
When I talk about being a Christian, this excitement that I show,
Is because I have realized that heaven is my home!

I Pity Your Blackened Heart

You believe in God; you believe in heaven and hell,
But you don't believe the Bible, and you can do what you want as well.
That's the definition of a Satanist, and the devil believes the same.
That's why Jesus Christ, in human form, came.
You're just like the Pharisees; hypocrite is the word.
If you think you're going to heaven, that is really so absurd.
You're spitting out blasphemy with everything you say.
You could have been forgiven, but for that, there is no way.
I wondered and was bewildered—what were you doing all this for?
Then I realized that the problem was that you're evil to the core.
You may not like or agree with what I have said,
But it's all plain and simple, and it's written in red!

Reality Cannot Be Fake

The message from Jesus was one of pure love.
It came from the Father in the heavens above.
Love your neighbor as yourself was; His number one command,
Care for the poor and needy and lend a helping hand.
Trust in the Lord and change the evil ways.
Thank Him for your salvation and give Him all the praise.
Obey all the laws that Moses did give.
Imitating Jesus Christ is how you should live.
Have a heart for the widows and the orphans too,
If you say you are Christlike, this is what you should do.
You spent your life in darkness, now walk in the light.
It's easy to do just do what is right.
Accept Him as your Savior for goodness' sake.
Make the right decision and don't be fake!

Moving from Darkness to Light

Hiding in the shadows, staying far behind,
Keeping out of sight, closed within my mind.
I may not know where I'm going, but I know where I've been.
What I have to do now is stay away from sin.
If you give the devil an inch, he'll try to take a mile.
He'll work his way in and stay with you for a while.
He'll bring misery and darkness everywhere you go,
Taking over your life before you even know.
We should stay alert, or he will try to stay.
Remain in the Word because Jesus is the way.
There is still hope, and I can tell you how,
To beat him at his game and make him flee right now.
Go to God in prayer for mercy and for grace.
Say, "In the name of Jesus, devil leave this place."
You can ask the Lord to surround you with His love.
Then you will have the peace that comes from God above!

Mining for Coal

A gaze upon the morning sun, my thoughts are only of you.
The beauty of the sight I see can only be compared to a few.
One is your eyes, the window to your soul.
Our future is what I see in them; that story is left untold.
Two is your smile, which melts this heart of mine.
It's like apples and oranges as to how bright the sun does shine.
Third is your beauty which everyone can see,
But what's hidden in its amazement is what it does to me.
From the first moment I saw you, girl, I knew right from the start,
You were put here on this earth for me to love with all my heart.
I love you with all I have inside my mind, body, and soul.
Each morning, I thank our Lord that I found me a diamond just mining for coal!

This Is Who I Am

My name is Wyatt, but they call me Sarge.
I'm sitting in jail, so I'm not in charge.
I like to encourage and give out hope.
It may not be much, but it helps others cope.
I'm still sitting here because I couldn't make bail.
And if your time is up, they just say, "Oh well."
I will always proclaim that Jesus is Lord.
And no matter what, I live by the sword.
That's the Word of God in case you didn't know.
Love and compassion is what I always show.
I lend a helping hand to everyone I meet,
I'm the same in here as I am on the street.
Everyone knows that my word is my bond,
And like it or not, with the truth, I'll respond.
Since I gave my life to Christ, I have always shown
That God is my Master, and heaven is my home!

A Cry for Mercy

Where am I going? Where have I been?
What state of mind am I really in?
Why am I living? Why am I numb?
If I pray for the Spirit, will He still come?
Why should I pray for myself anyway?
I'm not sure He hears those prayers today.
I see when He answers my prayers for others,
But when it comes to me, He doesn't like to be bothered.
I'm dying from what I call an issue of blood.
It's been over a year that it flows like a flood.
Darker and darker, it begins to appear.
No matter what I say, no one wants to hear.
What do I do now that I feel all alone?
Like no one really cares about all the pain that I've known.
My pleas for help are like dust in the wind,
They go in one ear and out the other again.
All I hear is you know we hurt too,
So I just pray for them—it's all I know to do.
If no one cares for anyone else anymore,
Why do they call themselves Christians for?
I'm sinking into a deep, dark, isolated place.
Lord, I'm praying for your mercy and your grace.
You say that my sins you have erased,
So please answer my prayers while I seek Your face!

What Christlike Means

Say what you mean and mean what you say.
You should keep your word if you want respect today.
It's important that you pay your debts—what you owe.
The essence of a man in time he will show.
If you're cruel to others, that's what you'll get in return.
But if you seek God's face, love is what you'll learn.
Just when you think that you are done,
God reminds you that He is number one.
Love is in the heart of a generous soul.
God's grace and mercy will make you whole.
Peace is in the mind of one who loves the Lord.
A righteous person lives according to the sword.
Kindness and goodness come from a Christian who is true.
Put your trust in God, and He'll show you what to do.
Accept Christ as your Savior, and your sins, He'll erase.
He will change your life as you seek His face.
These are promises from God; we are told.
Follow them, go to heaven, and walk the streets of gold!

My Joyous Peaceful Treasure

Today is the day that you became my wife,
And now we're tougher for a more peaceful life.
No more depression or feeling alone,
And now our devotion has truly been shown.
We will overcome anything that comes near,
And with me by your side, you will never have to fear.
With you on my arm, it's like an angel in my ear.
You urge me to do right, and that is so clear.
The heart that you show makes my heart sing,
And I am so proud to call you, Mrs. King!

A Heart of Appreciation

Today you have turned thirty years old,
Just like Momma, you can be bold.
You think of others every day,
And you don't care what people say.
Your heart is beyond all measure,
And that makes you a golden treasure.
That means you deserve what you like.
People can accept it or take a hike.
You are a jewel, and this we know.
Love and joy are what you show.
Everyone around knows this is true,
So we all say Andrea, happy birthday to you!

Man of God to Follow

Today you're forty-seven but still not old,
"But that's just a number" is what I am told.
The love of God shines through you; it's plain to see.
I hope the light of Jesus like you shines in me.
Your home is a peaceful sanctuary for all,
And you have a goal that fulfills God's call.
You read the Word, and that's how you lead,
And you're there for your family when they're in need.
You can count on that; we all want to say,
"We love you, proud of you, and happy birthday!"

No Doubt

I live my life as real as I can.
No matter the problem, I always have a plan.
It may not be plain for others to see,
But it's brought to the table when it needs to be.
My heart to help people, I know it shows,
It's not always safe, but that's how it flows.
I try to bring peace at all times to my home,
And ready to do battle when the devil does roam.
My past is under the blood, and it makes me shout,
And the light of God shines through me, and I serve only Him, there is no doubt!

My Heart Today

Loving now my new life,
And even more my final wife.
When all the woes weighed us down,
Which made our faces always frown.
We're now on solid ground,
Our love for each other is a great sound.
Our next long haul will make a family,
And from this darkness, we'll be smiling.
I can't wait to create a new mom,
With family together, loving some.
"We'll all pull through" is what we should say,
Just like that, I wanna be that way.
Love, life, happiness, and peace,
That I wish for all who please!

True Protectors of Peace

I am a police officer; my job is to protect and serve,
And now instead of doing my job, I have to deal with this pompous perve.
This is what I call him because that is what he's charged,
But if I knew reality, knowing him would actually be hard.
He has a heart that is made of gold,
Yet he also has a power that is truly untold.
He could defeat many although his size is small,
Yet he tries to take people in, and he does this for all.
He doesn't discriminate by what they have done,
But when it comes to battle, he can be defeated by none.
Now if I truly went by the oath I have sworn,
I would look at how this guy was truly born.
I should look into the soul of this man that I know
And really understand what his heart does show.
My job is much more than putting people in jail,
But also knowing the difference between evil and good as well.
I am not supposed to think about putting people behind a wall,
But know that I should be helping the weak—that's what makes me an officer of the law!

You Have No Idea

When you look at my life, what do you see?
Do you see what they want, or who I am to me?
My life has been a blast—I've traveled from East to West,
But what I have to say is something I must confess.
I confess that I've been a jerk for a good portion of my days.
I confess that I'm not proud of many of my ways.
But my heart's not as black as some would have you believe.
I'm not saying that I'm perfect; I don't want you deceived.
If you've never tried to know me, you don't have a clue,
So give me just a minute to enlighten you.
My goal in life has always been to make others smile,
And I have pondered and even studied how to do this for a while.
And I have found many ways to do just this,
But everyone is different, so it's always hit or miss.
My heart always breaks when I see someone cry.
I don't even have to know them, and I never realized why.
Am I just weak, or do I care that much?
How can I be bad if I love as such?
If my heart is that black, then why should I live?
If all I've done is useless, what more do I have to give?
Is there hope for redemption? Can someone tell me now?
Can I make someone listen? Will someone show me how?

I'm at the end of my rope; my mind is shutting down.
I'm tired of giving it my all and looking like a clown.
I've looked to politicians; I've looked high and low.
So now I'm at a loss and don't know where to go.
If you've never gotten to know me deep into my soul,
Then you have no idea Wyatt as a whole!

I Know Your Name

When the darkness of evil shows its might,
The grace of God shines with the light.
When the hatred of man drags you down,
The love of Jesus will always abound.
When depression makes itself known,
The mercy of God will always be shown.
When troubles are made so clear,
That's when Jesus will show He's near.
When people are telling you that you are in danger,
Jesus is telling you, "I was born in a manger."
When people are telling you that Jesus doesn't save,
Jesus is telling you, "I rose from the grave."
Jesus is telling you that "this ain't no game,
Because you are my child, and I know your name!"

Truth Between Genesis and Revelation

Disaster everywhere I look in this world.
All over is hate and insults hurled.
No one cares or thinks with their heart.
With all of our words, we tear each other apart.
Can't we take a moment to see what is real,
To understand what someone else might feel?
Can we look deeper into the soul?
Maybe what we find could make us whole.
What we seek could be only a heartbeat away,
So search someone else's suffering today.
Yes, it means I'll have to be quiet to see,
What's important to you instead of me.
If we all were serious, would it be so absurd,
To search for love and peace look to His word?

Walking on a Cloud

When I think of my grandmother, I think of peace,
Which helps my pain and grief to release.
I think of helping others because she was always there,
And I try to remember that she's with Jesus in the air.
She tried to remind everyone of our Lord,
That if we are family, we should live in one accord.
Walk in love and forgive those who hurt,
Because one day, we all will return to the dirt.
God is our shepherd, and He walks with us all the way,
So we should give Him thanks every single day.
Be slow to anger and keep Jesus in your heart,
Raise your children in the Lord, and they will never depart.
Don't forget we're all human, so mistakes we're allowed,
Because what's important is that in the end, we walk with God on a cloud!

Our Love Still Holds

Well, here we are again on another Valentine's Day,
So now my heart will tell my mouth what to say.
See it's not really hard to tell you how I feel,
To explain to you how you made my love seal.
See, you took my hand but not before my heart,
And all you've asked of me is just to do my part.
After three months of marriage and four and a half years together,
Our bond with each other has become as tough as leather.
We know each other's pain, we know each other's faults,
We know each other's pleasures, and also each other's thoughts.
I love you for everything that we are.
I hope that our love with each other will go far.
I am a lucky man to have you as my wife,
And I will try to be the man you deserve for life.
To show that you'll keep me just as a sign,
Gimme a big luscious kiss and tell me you'll be my valentine!

About the Author

Wyatt is a born-again Christian, inspired by God to write poetry to inspire the world to lead a better, more productive life, but his ultimate goal and hope is to be a lighthouse to others so that they will turn their lives and hearts over to the Lord. His poetry and the light that he shines toward others have led at least twenty wayward men in jail to the Lord and turned at least three from the idea of suicide. He is from Tennessee, where he lives with his wife, Shirley, and his mother, Janice. He attends Experience Christian Church (ECC) in Murfreesboro. He is also a proud father of four beautiful grown daughters—Kaleigh, Courtney, Harley, and Elysha. He also has ten grandchildren. He has proudly served his country in the air force and the army. So his travels and experiences in life are what he uses to do most of his writing, hoping it will inspire everyone to continue with hope and faith in God that He will guide their path to a better way. His hobbies include disc golf, billiards, darts, walking through the woods, and a passion for music (i.e. bass guitar, singing, drums, and listening to various genres of Christian music [i.e. gospel, rap, country, rock, and metal]).